The Price of Gold

MIRIAM WADDINGTON

Toronto
Oxford University Press
1976

Some of these poems were first published in *Ariel, artscanada, Canadian Forum, Canadian Literature, Descant, Impulse, Journal of Canadian Studies, Literary Half-Yearly, Modern Poetry Studies, Queen's Quarterly, The Tamarack Review, The Globe and Mail, Toronto Star, Poetry London, Saturday Night, Waves, Windsor Review*, and were broadcast on CBC Anthology, CBC School Broadcasts, and CBC Ideas. 'Ten Years and More' appeared in *Best Poems of 1974* (selected from periodicals in English) where it was awarded one of the three annual Borestone Mountain Poetry Awards.

Ten poems are reprinted from earlier out-of-print books: 'Before I Go', 'Quiet', 'What is a Canadian', 'Portrait', 'The Wheel', 'In Exile', 'Trumpets', 'Spring on the Bay of Quinte' from *Call Them Canadians;* 'Someone Who Used to Have Someone' from *Say Yes;* 'The Bower' from *Dream Telescope*.

Publication of this book was assisted by the Canada Council

FOR ADELE AND DMITRI

© Miriam Waddington 1976

Poetry by Miriam Waddington

Green World
The Second Silence
The Season's Lovers
The Glass Trumpet
Call Them Canadians
Say Yes
Driving Home
Dream Telescope

ISBN 19-5402650

1234-9876

Printed in Canada by John Deyell Limited

PR5¬
9199.3
W3
P7
239243l

Contents

CONTENTS

CONTENTS

1 Rivers

We are not one but two
we are not two but four
we are not four but many
sometimes we are not any

WHAT THE ANGEL SAID

Caedmon dreamed
that an angel
came to him and
said: *sing* and
he awoke and sang.

I dreamed that
a man in a white
shirt sewn with
stars rose out
of the scrolls

of the snowy sea
and the angel
turned to me and
said: *love* and I
awoke and loved.

BY THE SEA: FOR A. M. KLEIN

His grief it fell and fell;
he mourned that his brain
could never be like new --
a seamless whole again.

He polished it with spit
and sealed the cracks with glue,
he pinned it to the air --
yet away it flew.

He caught it in a net
of silken words and wit,
but his broken brain
was fragmented and split.

He quilted it with grass
and anchored it with ships,
he sailed tilting words,
they foundered on his lips.

He dropped a silver line
into the tides of verse,
and found his broken brain
had hooked it to a curse.

So he called the angels down
from balconies of sky,
they emptied out his life,
they would not let him die.

Then someone drained the ponds
in his unlettered land,
and strangers hid the road
beneath a mile of sand,

Apollo's golden ear
was sealed against his cries,
his lonely broken brain
was barred from paradise.

His grief it falls and falls
on green fields and on white,
he rocks his broken brain
that never mended right,

And sings his silent song
to earth and tree and stone;
we hear it when we hear
the rain beat on the stone.

The rain beats on the stone:
but how many recognize
his broken brain, his fear,
are nothing but our own?

LITTLE PRAIRIE PICTURES

1

The whisper
of shape
or the color
of quiet
against no
boundaries.

2

Through trees
of space
distance leans
in closer.

3

White is folded
but not in squares
it has climbed
its own ladder
to the sun.

4

The forest
has turned
to stone the
lake sinks

into mirage
we leave
no footprints.

5

There is
no sun
in these mute
places only
unlighted dumbness
a kind of
blind glimpse
a brush of
what is left
when nothing
is left.

6

Slopes of
lateness
tilt the world
when the world
is tired
and sleeps
quietly
on its own axis.

7

I like
the soft hush
that circles
this sleep.

GRAND MANAN SKETCHES

1

The island
lies in perpetual
August you have
to expect storms
and hurricanes
also strong
sunlight slanting
across triangles
of rock glossy
and black as
seals

Here even
the rocks
are alive and
intelligent

2

In town
I entice monarch
and other butterflies
by planting milkweed
among the flowers

In Grand Manan
I don't need
such enticements, the
butterflies, monarch
and swallow-tail,
crowd in skimming
through spruces

drinking the daisies
and dipping their
wings into the
rosy flames of the
fireweed

3

Nothing
burns them
in this bright
light everything
moves to water
except me
who am motionless
stunned to stillness
covered with
gold dust

4

Look how
I am hanging
like a bird from
midsummer
golden
in sky space

5

And look
how I am
burning
burning away
the distance
of water of
sun of
island

RIVERS

I wasted my life looking
for dammed-up rivers
and old stone quarries
to swim in; all for the
sake of gravel, the dry
burn of sun, even the
taste of yellow water
foaming from clayholes.

I forgot that I never
liked the stillness of
lakes the windless weather
of cities until you came
on your way back from
the province of deltas
the accent of wheat still
heavy in your voice.

You came from the swampy
borders of dry riverbeds,
dragging seaweed into the
house, shedding dry blades
from the ancient grasslands,
and in your eyes I saw,
pebbly, dark, mysterious,
all the rivers of my life.

FOREST POEM

I am alone now
in the tall forest;
I tread the water
of your absence.

More bitter to me
than salt is the
world emptied of
your meaning and

Who will now kindle
the lights for me
or wrap up the evening
in its white shawl?

DIVINATIONS

1

You are new as
the uncoiling fern
springtime in a pot
of green paint.

2

Do you ever feel
your mortality or do
all your lovers
die from your kisses?

3

When you stop
looking in mirrors
a fairy godmother will
come and your heart
will surely heal.

LEGENDS

1

Blinded I
kiss your mouth
in bazaars of
ice, saloons of
snow, the dark cave
of winter, glad
that your eyes
are open.

2

I move
through the grassy
lands inside
your lovegiving.

3

And search the
dark for your
face among a
thousand faces,
they enclose
the night in
a half-circle;
the birch bow is
in the hands of
the bone hunter.

4

You step forward
you circle
half of me and
become an ancient
arrow in the
trough of rivers
shattering the
sun into a thousand
windows of
rain.

5

Even the
rain today
is full of
quivering
light.

6

I taste the sand
of summer
in your mouth;
wide beaches
roll back
the covers of
my life.

7

Your body
becomes
its own legend
of fire.

8

And I become
the legend of
earth
asleep in the
stillness of
earth.

ECSTASY

The pale net of her hair
blowing in spring
will not
shut out the world
nor will the green knee
of season
bend to his will;

These two
separated by a field
of growing wheat
and several cities
still incline to each other
and from their distance
merge
slight and brief
as clouds touching

BEFORE I GO

I have to hurry
                but before I go
I want to give you
the very first words
                of summer
and invent
            especially and only
                    for you
a completely new language
                  giddy
as butterflies
            burning
as prairie sunsets

But I have to hurry or
my words are not my words,
                  at dawn
I fall into a
            dumbness,
my words close,
              at noon
they scatter
and the newsboy gathers them
                    public
in at every corner
and calls them
              promiscuous
out to every comer

LEAVES

His body is a tree
hung with nests
of singing names
with leaves
of printed messages from
Chinese fortune cookies.

The tree sways
with the weight
of German Rosas
Austrian Ilses
Welsh Aprils and
North Atlantic Mays.

But the book of the desert
dried by mountain fires,
divided by Egypt waters,
the chapter of Miriam
hangs fortuneless, leaves
locked in stone.

DON'T SAY ANYTHING

For W.T.

Don't say anything
about my looks
the dresses I wear
whether I smile
or not;
don't be glad to
see me don't
kiss me don't
pretend I'm
a heroine I'll
be satisfied if
you just pretend
you're human.

AN UNLIBERATED WOMAN
SEEN FROM A DISTANCE

I suppose I am
thinking of wooden
houses in Moscow
because I want to be
like Tolstoy's Natasha
I want to burn with
love and don't want
to remember your
silence or those
cold stormy kisses
that swept me aside
like a wind

PROFILE OF AN
UNLIBERATED WOMAN

I was a dish
to be eaten off
to be broken
I suppose to
fall wherever
I fell I wish
I had been
more (or less)
breakable I
was blank
white un-
patterned
and I had
only the usual
contrariness
the irritating
resistence of
all inanimate
objects

A SPACE OF LOVE

By the gravity
of your eyes
I fell into a
space of love
your rosy voice
became the air
of my songs the
fires of ritual
destroyed darkness
and fell like
a rain on the
kingdom of unlisted
cities and your

presence flowered
there your presence
towered there your
presence circled
the eagles of light.

LONDON NIGHT

There was nothing
to remember;
only the beating
of your heart
and the beating
of wings on the
windowpane
and all the sorrow
that being a woman
asleep
beside a man
can bring.

Were they
angels
of the city or
Blake's chimney-
sweeps or were they
birds of London's
summer night?
There were no
angels in that
room there was
no fluttering
of wings.

There was only
an old woman
shaking her head
and sighing at

the years that lay
heavy in her
lap tangling
words and tying
them in a jumble
of cruel knots
and ragged torn
strings.

I slept uneasily
and dreamed of
Caedmon and his
angel: in my dream
I stood and sang
into an empty
city and there
was no one to
remember, no
mythic heroine,
no legendary
king.

Then I woke
blinded by the
darkness
of your arm
across my eyes,
imprisoned
by its heavy
locked gate
and chained
to a thousand
iron rings.

THE DARK LAKE

Our ghosts still sit there
on the stone bench in the garden
they are eating lunch under the statue
and they stare straight ahead
into the dark lake of the trees.

Our ghosts have noticed something
in the dark lake of the trees
it is a different season and they are
not the only ones in the garden,
this year the people are not kind.

Our ghosts sit there and stare ahead,
this year the people are not kind;
their eyes are fixed
on the lake of the dark trees
they do not see each other.

They sit on the stone bench
they do not see each other,
each one is looking inward and
each one is continually taking
the photograph of his own ghost.

SOMEONE WHO USED
TO HAVE SOMEONE

There used to be someone
to whom I could say do you
love me and be sure that the
answer would always be yes;
there used to be someone to
whom I could telephone and
be sure when the operator
said, do you accept the charges
the answer would always be yes;
but now there is no one to ask,
no one to telephone from the
strangeness of cities in the
lateness of nightness, now there
is no-one, always now no-one,
no someone no never at all.

Can you imagine what it is
like to live in a world where
there is no-one, now always no
no-one and never some some-
one to ask do you love me and
be sure that the answer would
always be yes?   I live in a world
where only the billboards are
always   they're twenty feet tall
and they circle the city, they
coax and caress me, they heat
me and cool me, they promise and
plead me with colour and comfort:

you can get to sleep with me
tonight (the me being ovaltine)
but who wants to get to sleep
with a cup of ovaltine, what
kind of sleep is that for some-
one who used to have someone
to ask do you love me and
be sure that the answer
would always be yes?

QUIET

Quiet as the world after midnight
quiet, quiet is my thought of you.

I wait till all the people are asleep
so my thought can touch you, you, only you.

let this be my poem to you
you, you you, only you.

BEAU—BELLE

I'm in love with a clerk
from Trois Rivières
who trills his r's
and slicks his hair;

He's smooth as a seal
his smile is jolly,
though my name is Miriam
he calls me Polly;

He sends me greetings
on golden cards
and mails me snapshots
of snowy yards;

I'm *mauvaise anglaise*--
this he forgives,
between us two
it's live-and-let-lives;

He's in his city,
I'm in mine,
we meet at Easter
on Bleury and Pine;

He calls me Polly,
I call him Patrice,
he says *Madame*
a votre service;

And I say *Monsieur*
dis-moi tu,
tu es poupé
and I love you.

THE THINGS
WE TALKED ABOUT

After seven years
when I saw that
between us everything
was going nowhere
my one-sided
devotion suddenly
ended.

When we first met
we used to talk
about art, later
we talked about
artists and
finally we talked
about his arthritis.

Of all the things
we ever talked about,
the one I enjoyed most
was his arthritis,
it at least was
personal and my
devotion had never
been to his mind,

It had been to
his dark rosy face
and his black eyes,
the like of which
were never before
and will never again
be seen on this
earth.

Love still lives
in a place
where the wind stands
and fiddles for
north country dances,
where the rabbits run
across morning lawns
their paws diamonded
with dew,
where the forsythia
bush studs with
flowers the golden
tiara of April
and the violins
everywhere
fill up with the
long grazing notes
of pastured
summer.

HARVEST

Every man
has a right
to his dream,
mine is a crop
of books so I
cultivate my papers
as if they were
lands, I plough
them and furrow,
sow words like
seeds, tend phrases
like plants,
thin them and
weed.

When summer
is over I
bring them
into the house,
their leaves shine
and glow and
all winter long
they burn me
with their dark
green fire.

THE SECRET OF OLD TREES

(For Tobie Steinhouse)

If I could just divine
the secret of old trees,
how to be
their vertical silences,
or if lying low
how to embrace
their caged green light,
their space,
or even let us say —
how to baste the grass
with pine needles and cones,
and then when it is done,
to serve the world up
as a delicious dish
of warm roasted earth
rolled in four-leaf clover,
and for dessert to drink,
like every summer comer,
from a giant loving cup
the liquor of the sun.

TALLNESS AND
DARKNESS

Wherever I travel
home has always
been your tallness
and darkness, but
was it tallness or
darkness that made
it more home and
why did I need both?

Your darkness is
pure Egypt; pyramids,
my little brother
Moses with his straight
brows and far-sighted
eyes; your tallness
is the other part,
northern steppes,
prairies,

My blue-eyed uncle
coming to Winnipeg
from the cruel snows
of White Russia, later
raising celery
on Point Pêlee, then
crossing an ocean
to lose himself in
the cold salty desert.

He is buried there
in a remote grave
without a marker,
he is sleeping there
under the restless
snows of Mount Harmon;

Those snows are
still always packed
tight around my heart;
when your darkness
descends the snows
melt and everything
hurts and grows.

NATIONAL TREASURES
IN HAVANA

In the south
circled by
round sun-faces
she stares; but
dreams of snow
and hears
the ice-songs
buried in dead
guitars.

The palm-dove
sings and sings
from the marshes
and for her
the drowned quays
unlock their hoard
of salt songs.

A man's voice
rides in on the
dark waves,
flows through the
curtained light
in a webbed net
of sound:

I love you he
sings, *with all*
my heart with
all my heart;
the words break
and scatter

over the water
until even the
silence
sings and the

Stillness
celebrates the
evening which
falls from the
sky's crevices
and fills the
empty streets
of Havana:

We love you,
sing the empty
streets of Havana,
with all our
hearts, with
all our past,
our slaves, our
dead poets, and
starved children,
we have declared
silence a national
treasure.

She listens and
circled by
round sun-faces
dreams of snow;
she hears the
ice-songs in
dead guitars.

2 Living Canadian

Every one is as their land is, as the climate is,
as the mountains and the rivers or their oceans
are . . . .

                              Gertrude Stein

WHAT IS A CANADIAN

What is a Canadian
anyway?   A mountain, a maple
leaf, a prairie, a Niagara fall,
a trail beside the Atlantic, a
bilingualism, a scarred mosaic,
a yes-no somehow-or-other maybe-
might-be should-be could-be
glacial shield, grain elevator,
empire daughter imperial order of
man woman child or what?

SNOW STORIES

When I was a child
I loved to hear
snow stories: how
travellers lost
their way and after
freezing became
warm, fell asleep
in the snow and
never woke up.

Or else travellers
were chased by
wolves on a snowy
night in December,
and a snowstorm
blinded them and the
wolves howled and
they lost the road
and never found it
again.

This Christmas
the snow story is
almost the same;
we travel and lose
our way, we fall
asleep and cannot
wake up, we are
under a spell cast
by the lies of winter.

We have let the
wolves of Chile
howl us off the road,
we stay asleep, we
do not stop for other
travellers, the light
hurts our eyes and
the truth gives us
a headache.

The potentates
of oil, the kings of
tar, the ministers
of sand and all the
presidents of wrong
entertain us every
night on television;
but we are still
mesmerized

By the snow stories
of childhood, gullible
to the fake gestures
of a foreign poet,
no one talks to his
neighbor anymore,
the heart of the world
is dark and cold.

The hearth of the world
is dark and cold,
this is a Christmas
no fire can warm.

THIS YEAR IN JERUSALEM

Other years Hannah
the woman who cleans
offices in Jerusalem
cursed the white sun
of Jerusalem because
it was not the green
sun of her village
in Poland.

This year that same
Hannah has something
to curse about; she
curses the Egyptians
and Assyerians who
killed the son she
brought to Jerusalem
from her village
in Poland.

And at dawn this year
the cats of Jerusalem
don't come anymore
to the steps of the
post-office to wait
for morning and the
charwomen to come
to work and feed them.

This year
even the cats know
there are too many
enemies.

Under what illusions
should she live when
from the tropical time
of flowers, heat and
filaments of vine,
humming birds, clipped
and eclipsed in budding
sentences and brilliant
sunshine lipped on
snowy scrolls of sea,
the stranger turned away
and left her a winter
of questions?
The dream ends here.

He came again in autumn
when young girls wore
purple daisies tangling
through their hair and
school-crossing guards
in phosphorescent shoes
clattered the white lines
and held up stop signs:
the markets in the suburbs
were loud with apples when
they broadcast the news
of quarantined Quebec
and freedoms left to lose
in civil Canada.
The place is here.

She still remembered
her own escape
from the man in the long
coat who followed her
for months in deepfreeze
country; she had to rend
her clothes in mourning,
cross an ocean, flood
her skin to find a space
rhythmic enough to
run in, she had to
fill her ears with a
lake of accents deep
enough to drown all
dishonest voices.
Their words are here.

Those blanching nights
hid terrorists and lovers,
they made him anonymous
of greying middle age;
no longer real he seemed
another continent, a legend
once dreamed by a girl
in a northern city as
she traced her scrolls
on frosty window panes.
Their names are here.

This was the time she
waited for; she had
no house where he could
live, no needs to fill,
no wish to give; she had
started to learn a new
language and moved in
a constant astonishment
of changing sounds; words
came and went, maps hung
and fell, edicts were issued,
violence grew, yet she knew
That peace was here.

She watched him leave;
his footsteps levelled
out in rain: and now
she treads dead names,
imagines distances --
absent-mindedly she reads
her country's history
in her own pulse and vein,
feels herself a blade of grass
in fields, in provinces;
and sometimes she hears
October dumbness
composing a refrain
for all its citizens:
The dream starts here.

DÉJÀ VU

That far terribly
northern city
I see when
I close my eyes
is it Winnipeg
or Leningrad?

Both have the same
skinny church
standing alone like
a cello in the snow,
and you can see
the same half-dozen
people on skis or
snowshoes making
their way across
the same flat
white park.

What's missing here
is the 18th century
architect who built
these houses with
their stucco fronts
and lace balconies,
also those 19th century
idlers squinting up
at the sun from behind
the curtains of their
second-storey windows
on the same cold
Saturday afternoons.

The iron gates
of the summer gardens
are locked, the snow
piles up its cushions
on empty benches and
the frost wraps itself
like a bridal wreath
around the lighted
smoking street lamps;

It is all
so much the same,
I can't tell
if this far terribly
northern city is
Winnipeg or is it
Leningrad?

HOW I SPENT THE YEAR
LISTENING TO THE
TEN O'CLOCK NEWS

Last year
there were executions
in Chile
bribes in
America no
transit for Jews
in Austria
and lies
lies everywhere.

The children
of Ireland are
also in the news,
they have become
hardened street
fighters some of
them murderers,
I ask myself
where will it
all end?

Of course
the interests of
Canadian citizens
(read corporations)
must be protected
at any cost no
matter how many
good men are
shot like dogs
in the streets

of Chile or
how many poets
die of a broken
heart.

They claim
the world is
changing getting
better they have
the moon walk
and moon walkers
to prove it,
but my brain
is bursting my
guts are twisted
I have too much
to say thank
God I am too old
to bear children.

THE LAND OF UTMOST

Here I am in the land
of Utmost (rock me daddy
eight injuns & a crowbar)
enlightened, *arrivée*,
ongekommen, at last, a blasted
greenhorn in violence, buggery,
non-standard spelling &
whatever Utmost they haven't
invented yet; what a land ($)
of wonders, sunrises, student
murders, entertainments!
wow! *loup garou!* mamma! ! !
in Grossinger's Catskills
they never leave you unfed
or unentertained for one
Rip-Van-Winkle graveyard
minute, United Jewish Appeal,
singing rabbis, (& they charge
a marathon,) but Utmost
is free, gloriously
stars and stripes
free for all!

(Can't be innovators
all, we can't innovate
all, or be all, or all be
Utmost) and even utmost is
not all mint tea & wild swooning—
pools & cats; edginess grows
weedy & tall in the west, growls,
keeps our Miss Estelle from Pip
in a Chas. Dickens' grip,
is not beautiful in case
you meet it face to face
in unclaimed arctic space —
may werewolves grunt you grace!
(I wouldn't want to find
the shoes that belong to
the feet that go with that
Utmost etc. face under my
bed in a dark light on
a midsummer pink night)
but don't go by me,
committed, sentenced
to first-class false-brass
middle-mass human-prison
mortality for life,
or maybe longer.

HUSBANDS

My husband had two wives,
me and she, but me was legal.
Signed, sealed, and twice
delivered, I cookered,
cleanered, polishered spoons,
floors, and children; her wasn't,
so she at nine drove up the
hill to hospital and job.
Well, now she's in, I'm out;
still childered, cookered,
cleanered but somewhat
tarnishered, I drive and drive
to live my loveless life
and swear to boss and job
my faith forever.

And that old termagent, my
tongue, is queen of nothing
now; has lately split, run off,
and begun to play it safe.
It likes to lie there low,
a frozen log in ice awaiting
spring's bright crack-up

to let go its drift of grief
and garbage; but my brain
stays loyal and knows its
loves and hates; endlessly
it calculates why him and me
and she did equal minus me;
and no matter how I add, I'm
left with nothing now except
to wonder how was lost the rich
and gleam (by grace of course
unearned) of love, and love's
dear increment.

LOVERS

Sam promises: *lose 20 lbs
and it's Dior-Givenchy all
the way* (meantime a weekend
in NY in some splotchy dark
hotel should keep her happy,
put her in the mood -- not like
his Gladdie-pie who sold the
family manse for 30 silver
condominiums without the wave
of wands or bat of eye or single
kibitzing goodbye--)
Oh what a tatty daddy to offer
his leftwing ladylove such
ulcerated sweets!   Yet Sam's
a certain style of lover,
a hemm-er and a haw-er, sugarless,
and instead of being a sigh-er,
Sam is alas, a cough-er:
noisy and acidulous
in passion's market-place,
he bids on his success
and makes the lowest offer.

FRIENDS

The postman is no kibitizer,
he gravely deals with fate,
brings bills from Eaton's
and regrets from Volvo:
their warranty won't cover . . .
also: Domtar won't re-roof.
Re fellowships: *your letter
comes too late:* re poetry:
*sorry, but we're overstocked
with women's verse* (forever)
the very hex and curse the
sow's ear in the purse of
literature since ever time began
and Adam was a man and Eve
was also ran.

And here's news from Leo,
my own gentleman, back from
Spain at last to find the snow
piled high and downtown traffic
stopped; the union still gives
trouble, committees stall,
so does the bi-and-bi, while he
for one would like to see
the language issue dropped.

Bad news, bad news, on every side!
Would you believe that Leo's tailor
died with Leo's measurements
inside his head?   We never know
what's apt to happen and although
money isn't everything, how will
things be, where will they go,
when us, our generation, win or lose,
fed up with curbing hell, at last
drops all the reins and everything
busts loose?

Don't worry Leo: uneasy only lies
the head that wears the crown;
let strikes rotate from coast to
coast and post-offices automate,
let ferries stop, make them, the people
wait while railways alternate;
we're out of it, or will be, pretty soon.
Think on these words dear Leo,
(they weren't written on the moon
but on this dear planet that spins
us silly): *death comes to everyone.*
Yrs. truly, Trilby.

I'm back
and the profile of
Jackson Pollock stares
at me from a catalogue
cover in the jumble
on my desk; he makes
me want to cry over
the disorder of
everything human.

On the campus I pass
strange and terrible
Englishmen; albino eyes
dry umbrellas, giant
shadows and on the
bland blind faces of
Americans I read my fate:
the politics of exile
in my own country.

Where are we all
heading for who disappear
into Central Square into
coffee-shop into book-
store who are swallowed
into bullet elevators,
shot out into classrooms,
who rifle history push
our way into the past?

I am walking back
to an English colony,
watch me change into
an American aspiration,
look, I'm whispering into
a Canadian answer-box,
and not even the profile
of Jackson Pollock, his
suffering or my own
anger can stop it, so
it's high time for me to be
feeling this low.

PUTTING ON
AND TAKING OFF

This putting on
and taking off
of worlds, smiles,
words, those
lectures in
red auditoriums
wired for blue
sound.

I don't want
to work
at language
anymore I
am tired of
thinking.

I want to lie
on my back in
a forest of
grass, just be
a grasshopper,
an ant, just
bend my jointed
legs and

Leap through
the jungle of
stems, or I
want to go
to sleep in a
picture-frame
inside a Lawren
Harris mountain.

Why doesn't
somebody put
me into a poem
where I could
just be and not
mean, where
I could just
keep mum, blank,
silent?

I don't want
above all to
talk, lecture,
be teacher, at
least not
for a while.

MORNING ON COOPER STREET

Eight o'clock: morning
on Cooper Street,
October sun falls
through half-fans and
anchors, lights the
stainedglass transoms
of rooming-houses.

The smell of yesterday's
frenchfries hangs outside
the quicklunch: across
the street the humming
machinery of the Sealtest
factory is forever churning
milk into cartons (you would
hardly believe this is a
scene in the seventies in
Ottawa the nation's capital.)

Except that the cars
are already parked
thick as rats outside
Mamma Mafia's cafe and
the bicycle repair shop
is open too (I wonder
if they really fix
bicycles and whose),
I pass a spastic man,

two old ladies with
shopping bags and a
dozen sleepy people
coming out of the rooms
of their rooming-houses.

They teeter, list, and
drift, spindly and dazed
in the morning traffic,
they are precarious as
the houses they live in,
and condemned to the same
development, a future
that has no room for
old things, no place
for living people.

I look around, listen,
take in these new omens
and old dangers; I'm
superstitious, I carry
amulets and lucky images:
I'm remembering
a clump of mushrooms blazing
yellowly in the woods
safe somewhere far
far away across the river.

PORTRAIT: OLD WOMAN

Old woman, cabbage queen,
gourd-tapper, fortune-
hunter in teacups —
the black plumes
of your hatboat
quiver in the wind
tremble with secret
piracy as your knowing
hand touches without
gloves the supreme
trophy of the world's
cargo — peppersquash.

When you come home
to your rooming house
with the reddest apple,
the most grooved most
crenellated peppersquash,
the other old ladies
will vote you the
prize for picking, you
will be snow-white and
rose-red, you will be
royal at last,
queening it in the
communal kitchen of
your rooming house.

THE WHEEL

How does the seed grow
in what city is the wheel
that turns the world,
Montreal or Winnipeg?
We do not know.

The best we know
is like the child asleep,
helpless, a face
with sorrows deep, the best
we have is that we're partly
old and partly young but

Best there is,
and this best we give:
to nature's question
our answer is:
turn the world and
shelter us, the wheel
is in the seed.

IN EXILE

We'll turn the animals
into a Noah's Ark
and to our new land
take spotted leghorns
mica mines black swans
and daisies of Michaelmas
to bloom on garbage dumps.

I am in exile,
therefore I dream
of new kingdoms
fabled as Oz and
fantastic as smoke-stacks
thrusting themselves
in a chorus of colour
from river to sky.

TRUMPETS

Through the dark trumpets
of north and south,
through the iron gates
of east and west,
the music blows loud,
clanging, hangs taut,
restrained, elegant
as an animal and

regular as moons
the city tides advance, are
trapped in sewers; traffic signs
are blind, the streets are
bare, the sound is turned off:
where are all the people?

POETS ARE STILL WRITING
POEMS ABOUT SPRING
AND HERE IS MINE:
SPRING

You're an ice-thing
a landslide, a whale,
a huge continental
cold nose-ring
dragging the world
by the tail into
a universal grandstand
before it ever thought
of being born.

Maybe not: maybe
you're more like
a fern all curled up
in a juicy green bud
that any minute now
is going to burst out
of the loamy seams
of this workaday lazy
earth into a fresh
fernfan.

You'll be festive
with lacey little
pinked edges cut
out with God's own
zigzag scissors and
his million laughs,
you'll be cagey
and cunning and
you'll brush your
fingery fronds fond
as whiskers against

everyone's bare
legs, and you'll touch
us all with little
barbs of hot prickly
light, and we'll be
dyed green by the
crowds of wildly
cheering fernfans
sitting in the packed
high galleries of summer.

SPRING ON THE BAY OF QUINTE

Hey, what's this?
Sand-colored riffled clay, pure
lake pleasure and such a bland blind
enterprise of sky (mercifully
without intelligence),
come on, baby orchards, hurry;
get up from the ploughed
and flooded fields,
keep out of those puddles
or your feet will get wet,
and your bark will be scalded;
don't you know
this is pneumonia weather?

POPULAR GEOGRAPHY

Miami is one big yellow
pantsuit where the ocean
is louder than the sighs
of old age; Chicago is
a huge hot gun sending
smoke into the sky for
1000 miles to Winnipeg;
New York is a bright sharp
hypodermic needle and the
Metropolitan Opera singing
Wagner on winter afternoons,
and my own Toronto is an
Eaton's charge account adding
to the music in a Henry Moore
skating rink; Montreal was
once an Iroquois city huddled
around a mountain under a cross
and now is the autoroute to
an Olympic dream; everything
has changed, all the cities
are different, but Manitoba
oh Manitoba, you are still
a beautiful green grain
elevator storing the sunlight
and growing out of the black
summer earth.

THE WIND IN
CHARLOTTETOWN

Early morning;
and the wind
is awake, he
lays his hands
on the shore and
his head on the
gulf lap of
red sand, of
pine needles.

The wind
murmurs love to
Jerusalem and love
to Charlottetown,
it makes no
difference to him
whether he's in
Jerusalem or
Charlottetown;

As long as he
can weave his
hands in and out
of the seasons,
as long as he
can knit up the
dogwood and drape
the forsythia
on the bosom of
old lady world.

His voice is
ancient and layered
like stone with
the grief of
Jerusalem and the
crying of birds on
the prairie wastes,
and his voice is
as old and sad
as the lament of
the folksinger

Alone and adrift
on Prince Edward Island.

TOURISTS

For travel
they buy the style
and luggage of
the country:
plastic shopping
bags or canvas
holdalls for their
greyhound trips;
they wear pants
and sweaters,
the latest
in sunglasses,
but their eyes
their eyes are
imprisoned in their
own legends.

They leave
bouquets of wonder
at all our historic
sites, yet their
eyes their eyes are
tranced and still,
and still elsewhere.

CHARLOTTETOWN

It rains a lot
in Charlottetown
a queen city with
English corners
and streets cut
on the bias
a lady of a city
with an English
accent with a lace
cap and wooden
white houses like
buttons on her
black old bosom.

WOMEN

For a thousand years
in a thousand cities
we have lived in
images dreamed by
others, we have been
lamp-lighters in houses,
bulb-changers in
apartments, spinners
of wool in tents, weavers
of linen in cottages,
and foreladies of
nylon in factories.

We were always
the floor-washers and
the jam-makers the
child-bearers and
the lullaby-singers,
yet our namelessness
was everywhere and
our names were written
always in wind, posted
only on air.

Now the winds blow
old images off the
mind's pages and we
are no more the face
in the picture but
the hand making the
picture, we are no more
the watery song above
the wind's waters but
the source of the waters
flowing back to the waters.

Our voices have healed
from the fever of silence,
they bring from the waters
the health of the morning,
we are mapping adventures
by the light of the future,

we are carving our names
in time's forest of stone.

ARTISTS AND OLD CHAIRS

For Helen Duffy

A puff of wind
a stretch of sky
a rush of air --
and Helen
who commands the stars
and planets
now commands
a chair.

Old and whiskered
its stuffings
thinning --
it wakes up
one morning
on the junkman's truck
alive and even
grinning.

Whoosh and thump!
It lands
in Helen's garden
with a mighty bump;
and there among
three birds two
squirrels five
marigolds an orange
cat and this
old friend,
the chair decides
that life's not over yet,
it's not the end.

Helen's garden
is nice, the company
likewise: three
birds two squirrels
five marigolds
an orange cat and
this old friend
are quite enough
to make the chair
forget
the leaky huts and
muddy humps of
the world's worst
garbage dumps.

The chair
looks on benign
and sees
the scarlet runner
climb and
turn somersaults
on its own vine;
sees also how
it tickles windows
here and there
and how
its curly tendrils
defy all gravity
to lean on
simply air.

That's why the chair
decides
that nothing dies
or ends,
it only changes,
especially
when artists bring
their loving looks
to rest upon old things
and there discover
in such unlikely places
as rocky earthbound faces,
the eternal lineaments
of the transforming lover.

OLD CHAIR SONG

Knots and crosses,
thread and leather,
cut your losses
stitch a feather.

Knots and crosses
dot your i's
baste your losses
with your sighs.

Mend what's broken
make old new,
forms are false
but shapes are true.

So flash your thimble
push your luck,
if you win a chicken
lose a duck;

If you find a chair
that's old yet new,
it might teach you
how chairs grew

From knots and crosses
silk and tweed,
so close your eyes
and twist a bead;

Ask a riddle,
turn your head,
and you might learn
to raise the dead.

I TAKE MY SEAT
IN THE THEATRE

Look--
it's carnival time
in market square!
Here come
the musicians,
drum-beats, noise,
agitation:
the clatter
is deafening.

And here come
the masked dancers,
hands flying --
windmills:
heads rising --
towers: and hats
dipping, circling,
laced with
little windows,
motions
that lean out
of winter,
motions in a
medley of broken
mirrors reflecting
summer.

Beyond their masks
the dancers
are dancing out
the most ordinary

rituals; they
lunge, plunge,
spar, dodge,
(by day the chief
dancer is clerk
in the village
store) but here
he's bad-man tiger
against good-man
elephant, he's
stripe against
circle, sinister
against simple.

And now
one of them
shoots a silver
arrow into
the dust; tiger-man
folds his hands
over his heart
and drops dead among
the sunflower seeds
in market square.

Without warning
the princess
runs in; hurray!
All is well on
this side of
her rosy mask,
she holds a
bouquet and she

hangs a tinsel
wreath around the
neck of good-man
elephant.

Drum-beats; noise;
agitation;
the clatter is
deafening; the
ending is only
the return to
all the beginnings,
and no one sees
or looks
at the dead man
still lying in
the dust of
market square;

Except me
who am the people,
always
summoned from
everywhere to
watch everything
I stand around
and gossip
with neighbors
in the dusty square,
until night
falls
and the drumbeats
fade away and
stop forever.

AFTERNOON ON
GRAND MANAN

I sit at a table
on a small island
off the New Brunswick
coast doing nothing
thinking about
nothing.

It is Thursday
afternoon the light
on Swallow-Tail
comes and goes puts
away darkness and
like a good housewife
sweeps the sea,
the foghorn cuts
the mist and
rhythmically laments
the anonymous
dead.

At the wharf
the fishing boats are
back they have brought
in the haddock they have
filleted the pollock
and tomorrow they will
untie the herring nets,
the green-bordered boats
will empty the weirs.

(All summer
a man cuts birch trees
for the weir poles
his stories entertain
the tourists) but
the weather-man
is the only one who
can tell fortunes
or make prophecies,
the rest of us
pick berries and read
our dream books.

3 The Cave

We see in dead of dark
and find the face of night
we touch the side of day
and grasp the edge of light

TWO TREES

We all know
the tree of life
its tassels and
flowers,
its strong root
that sings and burns
in the centre
of everything.

But what of
the tree of death
that has been waiting
all winter,
waiting and sleeping,
sleeping and waiting,
in the centre
of everything?

In spring
it will burst
from a richness of
leaves
they will whisper
and sing: *come
come, come.*

They will whisper
and sing,
whisper and wait,
then cover us all
with their rich
dark shade
in the centre
of everything.

THE PRICE OF GOLD

The price of gold
is the same in Merida
as in Montreal but in
Amsterdam diamonds are
cheaper than in Toronto
or Capetown.

A wife costs more in
America than in Egypt,
and it takes less to bribe
an official in Hungary
than a bureaucrat in
Ottawa but in all these

Market-places, in every
corner of the world,
the price of death
is a hidden sum not
for barter or bribe but
meant to inscribe

On a secret scroll:
unlisted, unquoted,
not written or spoken,
its worth lies beyond
the talisman token,
and each of us knows

His own instant of death
by that strange sudden
thinning of blood and
of breath, and each
of us knows, at last,
when he's in it,

Where the doors open,
how the doors close.

SPRING

a loaf of bread
a jug of wine
and thou . . .

Here in this
complex province —
torn country
the bread we eat
is snow and
the wine we drink
is a Friday wind
blowing in from
somewhere
north of zero:

the thou in
the drowned fields
of my youth is the
darkening snapshot
of my dead husband
sitting among the
gravestones
in a Jewish cemetery
in Montreal.

When my husband
lay dying a mountain
a lake three
cities ten years
and more
lay between us:

There were our
sons my wounds
and theirs,
despair loneliness,
handfuls of un-
hammered nails
pictures never
hung all

The uneaten
meals and unslept
sleep; there was
retirement, and
worst of all
a green umbrella
he can never
take back.

I wrote him a
letter but all
I could think of
to say was: do you
remember Severn
River, the red canoe
with the sail
and lee-boards?

I was really saying
for the sake of our
youth and our love
I forgave him for
everything
and I was asking him
to forgive me too.

THE DEAD

The doubly dead
are harder to
reach than the
others like my
parents who were
always there
until they died
of time in their
own time;
but the doubly dead
who first went away
and then died,
like my husband --
those dead are
harder to reach:

Yet it was he
my dead husband
whose shadow
I glimpsed today
as I drove along
the sinking hills
and rising rivers
of the Gatineau;
and it was he
my dead husband,
who rose and called
to me from the
high rivers and the
drowned hills.

And it was he
my dead husband
whose face I saw
for the last time
before he turned
and walked away
into the darkness
that lies invisibly
across summer.

He walked away
taking himself and
our married years
into the darkness,
the same darkness
that looks out
at me now from
the eyes of our
two sons.

WIVES' TALES

When I married
my English
husband my Jewish
father said:
he'll get drunk
come home and
beat you,
you'll starve or
feed on green
pork stew --
well he didn't
and I didn't.

And my mother
being more
practical said:
if at least he
was a professor --
well he wasn't
and I was or
became.

Furthermore,
my mother said,
with a marriage
like that it's
plain curtains
for simple
you --

Well it was
curtains
in a way for a
while for me;
but for him
it was curtains
too and for him
forever and for
always.

ABSENCES

My father is dead
his wisdom is gone
from the world.

My husband is dead
his strength is gone
from the house.

His boat is lost
his oars broken
on a northern sea.

My bed is cold
my clothes lie empty
on a far shore.

THE BOWER

Love in your breast
will you build me a bower,
love in your hand
will you make me a nest,
and for my joy
will you raise me a tower
and make your heart
my flower?

For you my breast
will be no bower,
my hand will never
make your nest,
and for your joy
I'll raise no tower,
nor make my heart
your flower.

The autumn wind
will build your bower,
Algonquin lakes
make you a nest,
sorrow itself
will raise you a tower,
and death, death, will be
your flower.

A LOVER WHO KNOWS

The man with death
in his body knows
everything about death;
he knows how the walls
of laughter are
studded with skulls
in the crypts of Portugal,
he can follow
a gypsy on the dusty road,
and from the smoke
of her campfire,
from the smell of the
whiskey on her breath,
he can tell my fortune.

He has wings around
his face, love in his
eyes and he comes with
gentle kisses; he gives
me everything I want --
a sack full of words, a farm
north of the city,
perfect haircuts, safe-conduct
in five o'clock traffic --
but day and night he sleeps
in my grave and he never stops
calling me to hurry up
and come to bed.

ENDING

The big winds
of the world
have been called up
from sleep   they are
cross   shake thunder
and rain over the
city   spit out
teeth of ice from
their angry mouths.

I stand alone
in the great anteroom
no use now
even to be afraid
there is no one to
be afraid to anymore.

DOWNTOWN STREETS

There are still people
who write each other
intimate letters who
sing their personal arias
to an audience of white
paper; is it pain they
score, bursts of light they
note after a dark illness,

a childish jump, or some
mongrel dance-step in the
icicled rooms of snow?

Sometimes I still stand
outside a lighted window
on downtown streets (just
as I used to thirty years
ago) a woman sits at a
table writing intimate
letters, she is asking, *do
you really like the smell
of my perfume*, she is saying
*next time you come it will
be winter the season of
mandarin oranges.*

Standing there under
the window
I think I can hear
the sound
of her ghostly pen
moving across the page,
I think I can hear it
singing
in the downtown streets.

THE DAYS ARE SHORT

In September
the days are short,
and I think how
never did I love
my country so much
as now.

In October
the days are short,
and I think how
never did I regret
the summer so much
as now.

In November
the days are short,
and I think how
never did my words
fly south so much
as now

In December
when the days are short --
to look for
the country of my youth,
so blindly and so much
as now.

WHERE THE
NORTH WINDS LIVE

I long for
the transplanted
European village
the one
that became my
prairie city.

The north winds
lived there
they always
whistled me
clean
with a blow
of white polar
air.

They whistled
me clean and
they stripped
me bare then
they told me to
hurry
and gave me a
push with the paw
of a suddenly
humourous bear.

They gave me
a buss and a
blow and
with a spirally
flurry of snow,
they told me
to go from
the transplanted
village of snow,

To a land
where apples of gold
grow from a
golden hand,
and the touch
of a golden bear
warms
the summer air,
and forever
is always ever,
and forever is
always there.

THE CAVE

1

Back
back to the cave
of green light
and water
here is the self
here is the other
here
is the sky
without father
or mother
here
is the fire
and fear of
the father
here is the
mother the bringer
of water
here
is the brother
the healer
of hunger
and here is
the sister the
dancer diviner

2

The dragonfly
in the glacier the
fish that climbed
the slippery pier
here are
their traces their
watery faces
lit by the fire
of father and mother
by the ashes of self
by the birth of
the other and all
all are shadows
on shadowy walls
the shadowy laughter
of those
who come after

3

In the cave of
green light
where the self
is the other
and the mother
is father
and sister is
brother
where single

is double
and the double
is neither

the heart of
the earth is buried
forever
and the pulses
of water must
sound here forever
flowing back
to the cave
of green light
and water back
to the source
of their shadowy
laughter

4

Now the light
widens
from a crack
in the darkness
and the pulse
quickens through
miles of water
revealing the love
beyond lover
or healer

Revealing the hand
with its signs
and its wonders
writing bird
beak and claw
writing
ice mounds and ages
whose writing
has summoned
from the caves of
green light from
the flowing of
water
the shadowy figures
of those who come after
and their shadowy
laughter